I feel that the Bhagwad Gita is a treasure house of timeless wisdom, ancient knowledge and endless inspiration. And I believe that it can help anyone who seeks answers in life.

This book has been created for you to read aloud the stories about Krishna's life and teachings to your children and grandchildren. May this book help you introduce the younger generation to the rich heritage and tradition of India, and encourage them to enrich their lives.

Sudha Gupta

Bhagavad Gita

for children

Sudha Gupta

www.pegasusforkids.com

Published by Kuldeep Jain for B. Jain Publishers (P) Ltd., D-157, Sector 63, Noida - 201307, U.P.

Registered office: 1921/10, Chuna Mandi, Paharganj, New Delhi-110055

Printed in India

Contents

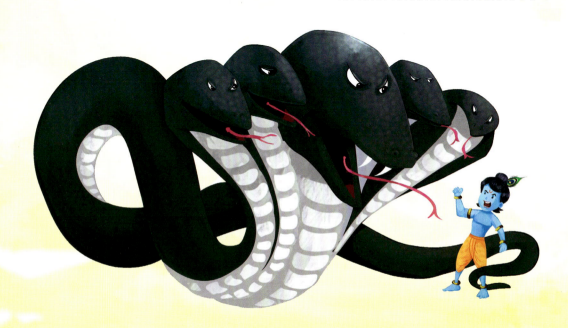

Birth of Krishna

About 5,000 years ago, Mathura, a small town in the present state of Uttar Pradesh, India, was under the rule of a tyrannical king named Kamsa.

Kamsa was so cruel that he imprisoned his father, Ugrasena, and declared himself the king of Mathura. Ugrasena was a kind and just ruler. Kamsa was just the opposite. It was a tough time for the people of Mathura to put up with Kamsa's extravagance and unfair rule. Above all this, he was constantly on war with other rulers of the Yadu dynasty. It had hampered the peace of Mathura.

Kamsa loved his cousin Devaki very much. He decided to marry his sister with Vasudeva. Vasudeva was a Yadu king and Kamsa had in his mind that his frequent wars with the Yadu dynasty would come to an end. Mathura was decorated beautifully and wore a festive look. Everyone was happy and in festive spirits.

Kamsa, cunning as he was, thought, 'Now, I'll have my hold on the kingdom of Vasudeva and rule the Yadus as per my own free will.'

After the wedding, Kamsa decided to drive the royal couple home himself to shower on them a kingly courtesy as was very common in those days. As soon as Kamsa took the reins of the wedding chariot in his hands, a divine voice thundered from the sky, 'Kamsa, you fool!

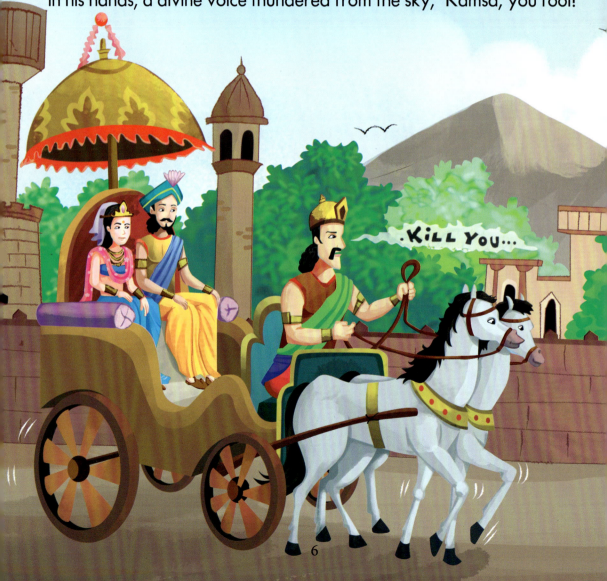

You don't know what ill fate is going to fall on you. By giving Devaki's hand to Vasudeva, you have signed your own death sentence.

The eighth son of Devaki will kill you!'

Hearing this, Kamsa froze with fear. He was very upset and furious. He immediately decided to kill Devaki at the spot. He thought, 'If I kill Devaki, no child can be born out of her!' Thinking so he drew out his sword and raised it to behead his cousin.

Vasudeva was horrified at this cruelty and fell on his knees. 'O Kamsa,' he pleaded, 'Please do not kill your sister! I shall personally surrender to you all the children she gives birth to so that the voice of the oracle does not come true.'

Hearing this, the evil king did not kill Devaki. He said, 'Then you will live in my palace as prisoners!' Vasudeva had no choice but to accept his decision. Kamsa laughed out loudly and spoke, 'Now, I'll see how the eighth son of Devaki would kill me. I'll kill him as soon as he is born!' He was content at the thought that the situation was under his control.

As was decided by Kamsa, Devaki and her husband Vasudeva were confined in the palace dungeon and kept under constant vigilance. Every time Devaki gave birth to a child in the dungeon, Kamsa killed the child. In this manner, he killed seven children born to Devaki. He turned a deaf ear to all the heart-rending cries of his sister.

'O brother, please spare the life of my children. They will never harm you, I promise,' pleaded Devaki sobbing, but in vain. Each time Kamsa killed the child mercilessly.

Nine years passed before Devaki got pregnant for the eighth time. Kamsa, troubled by the fear of his possible death, lost his appetite and slept poorly at night. 'I won't be at peace till the child is born!' he thought all the time.

In the palace dungeon, Vasudeva was trying his best to console his wife, but she was terrified. 'My eighth child will be born in a day,' she spoke crying bitterly. 'And my cruel and merciless inhumane brother will kill this one too. Oh mighty Lord, please save my child!'

The night soon ended and it was dawn. Devaki spent most of the day in tears. The day again ended and the dusk gave way to a terrible night, as had not been seen earlier in Mathura. It seemed that the whole world understood Devaki's pain and joined her in the mourning for the unborn child. The wind howled angrily and the sky seemed to have split apart to pour endless rains. Suddenly, there was an eerie silence. And then it was broken by the sound of the cry of the divine child. It was the voice of the eighth child, a son, born to Devaki at midnight.

As soon as the child was born, the prison was filled with a dazzling, blinding light. Devaki fainted at the sight and Vasudeva was mesmerized. The light converged into a sphere and the same voice of the oracle that scared Kamsa, now spoke to Vasudeva, 'Take this child across River Yamuna to Gokul. There, Nanda's wife Yashoda has just given birth to a daughter. Exchange your son for the girl child and return to the prison immediately, before anyone comes to know about the birth of this child.'

Hurriedly, without a word, Vasudeva picked up his newborn son following the divine advice. He felt very sad, as he had to separate the newborn child from his mother. But he knew that there was no other way to save his son.

Vasudeva felt very doubtful about how he would get out of the prison, unnoticed. There were a hundred soldiers on guard outside. And it was a dark, fearsome night. But what he saw astonished him greatly. All his problems were resolved one by one. As he approached the prison gate carrying the baby in a basket on his head, the doors opened on their own. Vasudeva came out slowly to find to his utter surprise that all the guards were sleeping!

It was raining heavily when Vasudeva left for Gokul. He soon approached the banks of River Yamuna. The river seemed to be seething with anger, due to fierce winds and rain. It looked alive and ready to devour anyone to set foot in it!

Vasudeva was full of fear. He was hesitating of stepping into the river. As if the river had sensed his fear, the turbulence subsided at once! Then a miracle happened. As soon as Vasudeva's feet touched the river, the flow became normal and Yamuna made way for the Lord.

To his amazement, Vasudeva saw a huge black snake raising its head from the waters behind him. Vasudeva was very scared, but soon realized that it meant no harm when he saw the serpent positioning its hood like an umbrella to save the newborn baby from rain.

This snake was none other than Sheshnag, the Snake-God, who is known to be the roofing canopy of Lord Vishnu and the newborn baby was the eighth incarnation of Lord Vishnu.

Vasudeva did not delay any further and proceeded in waist-deep water. And finally, he was able to cross the river and reach the opposite bank safely. From there he reached Gokul.

It was past midnight and the people of Gokul were fast asleep. Vasudeva had no trouble in entering Nanda's house because the doors were open.

Vasudeva, by this time, had realized that his child was really someone special. He was a divine child. All his fears vanished for he understood that when he could come this far, he would surely be able to complete the rest of his journey.

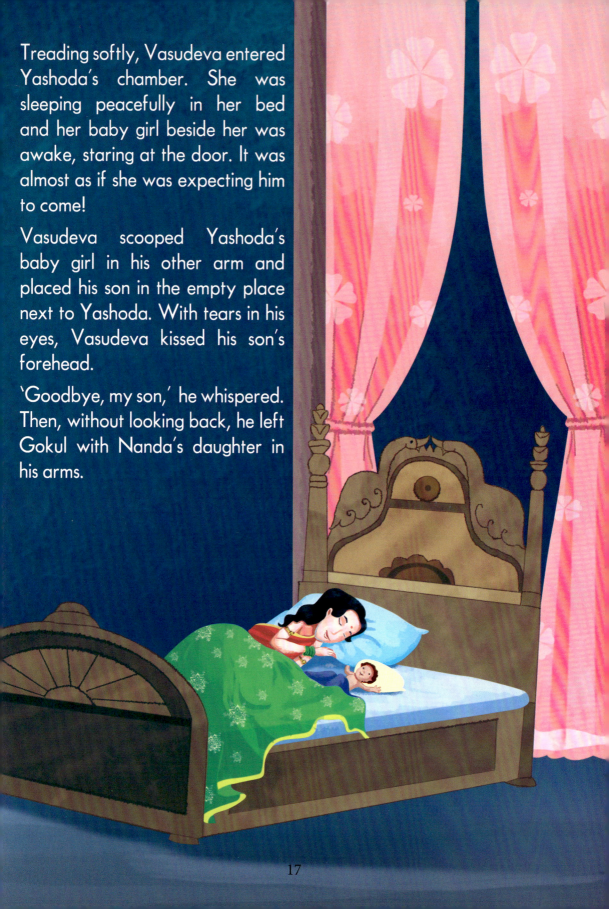

Treading softly, Vasudeva entered Yashoda's chamber. She was sleeping peacefully in her bed and her baby girl beside her was awake, staring at the door. It was almost as if she was expecting him to come!

Vasudeva scooped Yashoda's baby girl in his other arm and placed his son in the empty place next to Yashoda. With tears in his eyes, Vasudeva kissed his son's forehead.

'Goodbye, my son,' he whispered. Then, without looking back, he left Gokul with Nanda's daughter in his arms.

Like before, Sheshnag protected the child from the heavy rains and Vasudeva returned to the prison with the baby girl. He entered his dark cell and laid the baby by Devaki's side. As soon as the child felt the hard floor on her back, she cried loudly.

The guards suddenly awoke from their sleep and became aware that a baby was born. They rushed to Kamsa to give him the news. The eighth child, slayer of Kamsa, had taken birth!

The evil king was both pleased and afraid to hear the news. He was

pleased that he would finally kill the eighth child of his sister, but he was also afraid that he might not be able to do so.

Keeping aside all his fears, Kamsa rushed to the palace dungeon to execute the child who was said to be his slayer. He reached the dungeon in great anger. The palace guards trembled on seeing him. Kamsa entered the cell where his sister and her husband had been living for the past nine years. 'Where is he?' he roared at Devaki, who was weak from childbirth. 'Where's my slayer? Where is he?' thundered Kamsa.

Devaki had regained her consciousness only after Vasudeva had exchanged the babies. So Devaki thought that her eighth child was a daughter.

She appealed to her brother, 'O Kamsa, my brother, my eighth child is a girl, and not the son that the oracle warned you about. How can she harm you? Please let your niece live!'

Kamsa, as always, ignored her cries. He loved his life more than anything else in the world. He snatched the baby girl from Devaki's arms, and hurled the child against the prison wall.

But this time, the baby did not die. Instead, she flew up, and for a second, remained suspended in the air to the utter amazement of everyone present there. The prison was filled once again

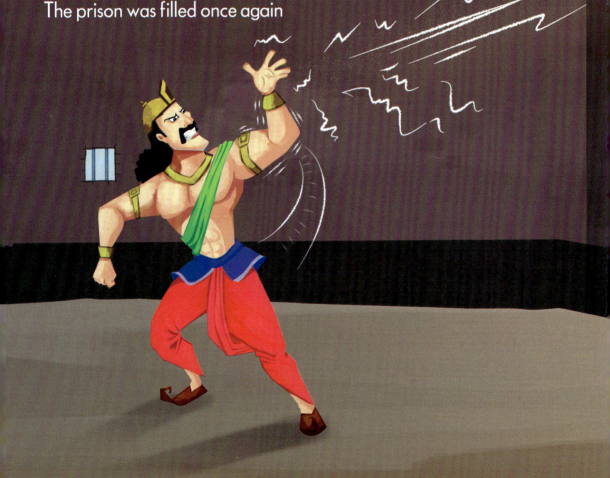

with a blinding light. Kamsa covered his face to shield himself. As the light subsided, they realized that the child had changed into a goddess!

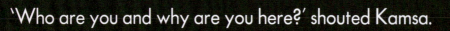

'Who are you and why are you here?' shouted Kamsa.

The eight-armed form of the divine goddess was dressed in shining garments and dazzling jewels. She looked in contempt and pity at the bewildered Kamsa.

She said, 'O foolish Kamsa, there is no force on heaven or earth that can kill me. So how can you, O wretched creature?

Your slayer is already born! He is now well and alive in a safe place. And one day, he will come and kill you!'

Saying so, she disappeared, leaving behind a terror-stricken Kamsa.

'What is happening? Now what shall I do to save myself?' wondered a shocked Kamsa at the turn of events.

Vasudeva then narrated what had happened that night to his wife. 'Our son is a divine being. He is the incarnation of Lord Vishnu. So do not lament, O Devaki!'

Devaki, though sad at the separation from her son, was happy for the baby. Both of them prayed to God that their son should not fall into the clutches of his evil uncle, Kamsa.

Meanwhile, there was great rejoicing in Gokul. The cowherds of Gokul were happy beyond measure. A new baby boy was born to their beloved Nanda!

The baby was named Krishna. Everyone in Nanda's family was very happy.

People of Gokul flocked to Nanda's house to see the divine baby boy and to offer gifts. Everyone noticed that the child was no ordinary one. His skin had a bluish hue and his eyes twinkled merrily. He did not cry and always had a smile for everyone.

Yashoda felt very proud of her newborn son who emitted so much divinity.

In this way, was born Lord Krishna, the Supreme God who is the creator of everyone. He was born to save everyone from terrible tyrants like Kamsa.

Krishna and Putana

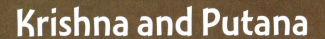

King Kamsa soon came to know that Krishna, his slayer, was alive and safe in Gokul. He immediately instructed Putana, a fierce demoness to kill baby Krishna.

Without wasting a single minute, Putana started for Gokul. She transformed herself into a beautiful woman and entered Yashoda's house.

The innocent cowherd women thought that Putana had come to see Krishna. Enamoured by her exquisite beauty, no one stopped her. Within no time, Putana found baby Krishna in his cradle. 'So, this tiny baby has caused so much fear! It is indeed strange,' she thought.

Putana took baby Krishna in her arms. Then she furtively tried to breast feed him. She had smeared a very powerful poison on her breasts. Putana was sure that as soon as the baby would suck her breast, he would die.

Baby Krishna took the nipple in his mouth in anger. He sucked out the milk-poison along with the life of the demoness. Putana fell down on the ground, crying, 'Please leave me, leave me!' While dying, Putana assumed her real form of a demoness. She fell to the ground with a thundering sound. Her fallen body extended up to twelve miles and smashed all the trees to pieces!

When the gopis came rushing, they saw that little Krishna was playing fearlessly in Putana's lap. They picked him up immediately. Mother Yashoda and other gopis present there realized that little Krishna was a divine child!

Infant Krishna

With bluish complexion, attractive look and mischievous nature, Yashoda's son became famous all around Gokul. Even at three months, he kicked and overturned a heavily loaded cart.

Once Trinavarta, a demon tried to kidnap him in the form of a whirlwind. But as he tried to carry him away, infant Krishna became heavier and heavier. Soon, Trinavarta had to let him go. Krishna, also called Nand-kishor and Yashoda-dulal, was extremely fond of butter and curd that the milkmaids at Gokul made. He was always crawling along or toddling over to the pots of milk products and stuffing handfuls into his mouth. Even when Yashoda tied them down from the ceiling, he would try and reach them, and then fell himself as well as broke the pots. To check him, one day Yashoda tied him to a heavy mortar. But Krishna easily dragged all that weight as he toddled outside. The mortar got caught between two tall trees but Krishna went on, the trees getting uprooted and pulled alongside. Both the trees were actually two gandharvas under a curse and now they were freed.

Krishna impressed everyone around him in that little village of cowherds and milkmaids. They came to realize that he was a wonder child.

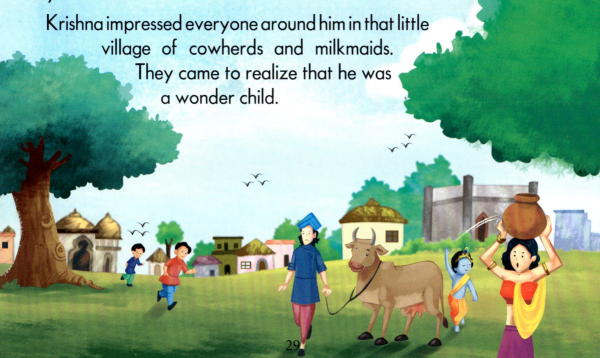

Krishna and Kalia

Days passed and Krishna grew up to be a fine boy. One day, it was cool and peaceful in the woods around Gokul. Now and then, a gentle breeze blew through the fresh, green leaves of the tall, majestic trees, as if playing with them. Cuckoos chirped cheerfully, butterflies chased each other and little crickets jumped here and there. Just then, there was a strange sound.

'Ssssssss!' hissed an evil voice, destroying all the merriment around.

It was a terrible serpent with many hoods named Kalia slowly coming out of its hiding place with its brood. They were poisonous creatures that poisoned the very ground they slithered on. As they moved, the grass under them turned black and the trees they passed by lost their green colour.

Kalia looked around himself. 'What a lovely place to stay with my family!' he thought and smiled to himself. 'Stop my children! This is our new home!' he commanded.

Hearing this, the wind, birds and trees were all troubled.

'No!' cried the wind, 'don't do this!' 'I can't breathe!' gasped a shocked peepal tree. Even the birds on the tree branches just reeled over and died due to the poison in the air. And so, the eastern part of the River Yamuna next to the village of Gokul began to slowly destroy.

Next day, the morning sun shone over Gokul. It was like any other day. Everyone went about their usual business. The village primarily consisted of cowherd tribes. They were getting ready to graze their cows in the nearby fields. Suddenly, there was a cry of fear from Nanda's house. An anxious crowd gathered outside Nanda's house to inquire what had happened. It was Yashoda, Nanda's wife who had shouted in fear.

She sat on the bed, her body shaking in fear.

'What happened, Yashoda?' Nanda asked worriedly.

'I had an awful dream,' shuddered Yashoda at the thought of it. 'I saw that a giant snake had coiled his enormous body around our little Krishna!'

'It was just a dream, Yashoda,' Nanda tried to pacify his wife, but in vain.

'I must see if my son is safe or not! Krishna! My son...where are you?' she called out.

Next moment, she heard the pitter-patter of a child's footsteps outside her room. Little Krishna peeped inside.

'Mother, did you call me?' he asked with a smile.

'Krishna, you will not go out anywhere today. Did you understand?' Yashoda said gently without wishing to alarm her son.

Krishna smiled mysteriously. It seemed to Yashoda as if he had a plan in his mind beyond any mortal understanding.

Ignoring Yashoda's words, Krishna ran out of his home. He ran fast through the streets of Gokul and arrived at the riverside hideout where his friends welcomed him. Then they started playing.

After some time, when they became tired, they climbed on a tree to rest in the tree house which Krishna and his friends had specially built for their adventures. But the tree was not strong enough to support so many children and it groaned under their weight.

Krishna felt bad. 'I wish we had a bigger tree to build a tree house on. We seem to be breaking this one!'

'I know where the biggest tree in Vrindavan is,' said Kusela, one of his closest friends. 'But my father said we should not go there.'

'We must go there! Come!' said Krishna merrily and ran towards the eastern direction. 'I want to build a better treetop hideout. And I need your help. Will you all come with me?'

Soon Krishna and his friends arrived at the eastern part of Vrindavan forest. But they were shocked at what they saw there. The place looked deserted and ghostly!

At a glance, the place looked good enough. The river had plenty of water and there was even a waterfall nearby. But only when the children went closer, they saw the terrible changes.

The water had a bluish colour. The grass around the river was not green anymore. It had turned black. There was a huge tree overlooking the river, but it was on the verge of dying. It had no leaves and its branches were all blackened. It seemed as if the whole place was cursed by some monstrous devil. There was a scary silence all around.

Krishna looked thoughtfully at Yamuna and then he turned to his friends.

'Well then, let's play with our ball!' he said as he grabbed the ball. He threw it at Kusela who was unable to catch it and let it slip into the river. The ball disappeared into the waters with a soft plop.

'Let me get it,' said Krishna and before his friends could stop him, he jumped into the strange, blue waters! 'Don't worry, I'll be back soon with the ball!' he assured them.

The water was very cold. Krishna swam deep down and found that all the plants were burnt and bent as if they were drenched in acid. He looked around to find the one responsible for it. He could see skeletons of small sea animals and fishes lying on the riverbed. An eerie silence prevailed all around. It seemed to be the Kingdom of Death.

Suddenly, little Krishna heard a strange hissing sound. 'Whoever did this is still here,' he thought.

Just then, a huge snake came sliding. It was Kalia. It was truly terrible to see his large body slithering in water. Raising his many hoods hissing loudly, he appeared before the little boy. The snake was surprised but also pleased to see Krishna.

'Ah! What do we see here, my children?' he asked mockingly.

'Food!' shouted his family in chorus, standing behind him.

'Yessssss...,' Kalia hissed wickedly. 'We do not get to taste humans often!' The next moment, Kalia lurched at Krishna.

Little Krishna, who had been expecting such a move, deftly jumped back and hid himself behind a rock. But Kalia moved at lightning speed and caught him. He coiled round Krishna and started to crush his body. Krishna, who was rather enjoying the fight, twisted his body and slipped out.

Kalia was stunned. It was impossible. How could this mere boy slip out of his grasp so easily? Nobody, no matter how big or small, had ever escaped from his deadly hold. Krishna, meanwhile, jumped over the rock and crouched low. He was in a playful mood and decided to tease the evil snake. Had the poor snake known who his opponent was, he would have never dared to try to devour Krishna.

Krishna was an incarnation of the Almighty God. He had come to earth to reward the good and punish the wicked. But Kalia did not know this and was determined on having Krishna as his meal.

As the snake came around a rock to catch him, Krishna quickly climbed over the rock and jumped on the snake's enormous hood. He firmly placed his foot on the snake's sensitive head and started to dance. And what a dance it was!

The whole Yamuna started to tremble as Krishna danced. The river animals and plants started to tremble. Even the fishes left alive stood still and watched Krishna dancing over Kalia's head.

'Stop dancing on my head!' Kalia screamed out in pain.

Krishna stopped dancing and slid lower near Kalia's face. He rained blows on his head and climbed back on his head to dance again.

Now, Kalia the mighty snake was truly afraid! He felt that surely the little boy was no ordinary child. As Krishna danced with more and more vigour, the snake felt his life was slowly leaving his body.

Kalia's wives pleaded, 'Oh, divine child, please don't kill our husband!'

'I will let him live if all of you promise to leave this place forever,' answered Krishna.

'But we are so safe in here!' cried Kalia. 'If we go out now, Garuda the giant eagle would surely kill us!'

'Go to Ramnaka, the snake-kingdom,' suggested Krishna. 'You and your family will not be attacked by any bird or beast till you reach there. That's my promise! Now off you go!'

Meanwhile, Krishna's friends ran back to Nanda's home and informed him about Krishna's underwater search for the ball.

Yashoda broke into tears. 'I had warned him not to go anywhere. Oh my Krishna... what will I do?'

Nanda too was scared. He called aloud for the other Gopalas. The village-folk rushed to the Yamuna-side. There was no sign of the little boy, anywhere. There was only a deathly silence everywhere.

'Krishna... my son! Where are you?' cried Nanda. 'Come out, please!'

Suddenly the waters of River Yamuna bubbled and rose above the tallest tree in the woods. The Gopalas moved back in fright and all of them looked in awe and fear as Krishna came out, dancing on top of a huge snake! The snake bent his head in respect as Krishna landed on the shore.

Content with Krishna's promise, Kalia gathered his brood and left Yamuna that very day. True to what Krishna said, neither birds nor beasts attacked the snake family on their way to Ramnaka.

The river regained its old richness and Krishna built his tree house on the now-green tree overlooking Yamuna. All the boys understood that Krishna was no ordinary child. Tales of his antics spread far and wide.

Krishna and Lord Indra

Once, it was the rainy season. The sky was overcast with clouds and the sun was smiling weakly behind dark clouds. Gokul, at that time, was a charming village. It was a lush green heaven with healthy vegetation. Everyone in the village was happy.

One day, Krishna woke up with a start. It was not yet morning, but there were loud sounds coming from the streets. Curious, he got up and peeped outside his window. A crowd had gathered before his house. Several men and women were sweeping the streets clean. The roads were being decorated with garlands and lamps. Krishna was surprised to see all this.

'Is there a festival today?' he wondered. But he couldn't remember any such occasion.

A little later, he left his home to take a bath in the river. While coming back, he saw his father Nanda overseeing the men in the streets.

'Father, what is happening on the streets?' Krishna asked his father.

'People are preparing to celebrate a festival to worship Lord Indra as he has given a generous rainfall this year! Everybody is happy with the fertile crops,' said Nanda.

'How do you know that Lord Indra is the one who's causing the rains, Father?' Krishna asked, frowning.

Up in the sky Lord Indra was listening to this conversation angrily. 'So that little cowherd boy dares to speak against me! ' he thought in fury. 'All these years, I heard their pleas and helped them to prosper. And this is what I get in return! It is time when they must know that the real God is here! I'll send the most severe rains and thunderstorms to Gokul,' he thought ominously. 'Let them see who saves them then!'

Lord Indra created the most dangerous clouds ever! 'Go and destroy Gokul!' he ordered. At once, the dark clouds raced towards Krishna's village.

It was afternoon; the people of Gokul were resting in their homes after lunch. Suddenly, they heard a terrible sound of thunder. What they saw outside alarmed them. The sky had darkened; the sun was nowhere to be seen. Instead, black terrible looking clouds had enveloped the whole place. The people of Gokul watched in fear and awe.

Young Krishna heard the frightened voices of the villagers. He was curious and came out of his house. The moment he stepped out, there was a great uproar and the black clouds poured rains over Nanda's house. It seemed as if this was what the monstrous clouds had been waiting for!

From Nanda's house, they quickly spread themselves over the rest of the village. Heavy rain came down in torrents, flushing away the cattle and the frail huts. The mere thatched roofs were no match for the terrible downpour.

The innocent people of Gokul ran in all directions to save their family and belongings. But nowhere could they take any shelter for nothing seemed to be strong enough against this mighty cloudburst. The poor, suffering people prayed for divine help.

'Do you see, son? This is no ordinary rainstorm. This seems to me to be the punishment of Lord Indra!' said Nanda miserably.

50

Krishna looked at the sky. 'Ah, vain Indra!' he thought in fury. 'You want to teach us a lesson, don't you? But first, you need one!'

Thinking so, Krishna laid a reassuring arm on his father's shoulder. Using his most commanding voice, he called out, 'O people of Gokul, look at me. Do not run. Do not panic!'

Everyone looked at Krishna miserably.

'This is all our fault!' somebody murmured. 'We insulted Indra and now he's punishing us,' commented another.

'What you say is right. This is indeed an evil plot of Lord Indra. But like before, Govardhan Mountain will help us once again. Come this way and I will show you how!' said Krishna smiling, as he led them to the mountain.

Krishna looked up and smiled at the clouds. And in a blink of an eye, he lifted Govardhan Mountain, like an umbrella over the people! People were stunned to see this. A boy had lifted a mountain on his little finger!

Up in heaven Indra was shocked. 'How can a mere child lift a mountain?' he wondered.

Just then, the voice of Lord Brahma was heard, 'You should have understood it by now, but you did not. Pride and arrogance have

52

clouded your common sense, Indra! Don't you know that Krishna is an incarnation of Lord Vishnu?'

Indra was greatly humbled. He stopped the rains at once. As a sign of apology, he ordered the clouds to shower rose petals from the sky!

Every resident of Gokul came to know that Krishna was a divine incarnation. 'Long live Krishna!' echoed everywhere.

Krishna and Bakasura

Kamsa, the wicked maternal uncle of Krishna, knew that Krishna was in Gokul. He also knew that he was the divine eighth child of Devaki who was destined to kill him. And so, Kamsa wanted to kill Krishna and thought of evil plans for doing so.

One day, he called the demon Bakasura.'Go at once and kill young Krishna,' commanded Kamsa.

Bakasura, decided to take the form of a huge bird to frighten young Krishna. One day, Krishna was playing with his friends in the forests of Vrindavan, when he saw a giant bird swooping down on them. Krishna at once understood that a demon was sent by Kamsa to kill him.

As the bird came closer, brave Krishna caught its beak and quickly got inside it. Inside the beak, Krishna wriggled around so much that Bakasura's beak was broken. Exhausted, Bakasura died after some time and fell to the ground.

'That serves you right Bakasura! You can never kill me,' said Krishna, satisfied.

Krishna's friends hugged him in joy.

Krishna and Aghasura

One day Krishna and his friends were playing when they came upon a mountain cave. This was actually the mouth of the brother of demoness Putana who had enlarged himself into an eight-mile long snake to kill the boys.

When the boys wanted to enter and explore the cave, Krishna became worried because he knew

it was one of Kamsa's tricks. He considered for a moment, and then decided to enter the cave himself. Demons all over the world became joyful when Krishna went inside. The gods, who had been hiding among the clouds to see what would happen, became distressed.

For a long time nothing happened. It seemed as if the snake-demon had killed Krishna. But a little later, Krishna grew larger and choked the demon to death.

Krishna thus saved his friends.

Krishna at Play

Krishna loved to dress up and go out with his friends with a flute on his lips, and tinkling anklets on his feet. He was friendly with everyone and never put on any airs because Nanda, his father, was the local chief.

Krishna was most dutiful and obedient towards his elder brother Balarama. Fair-complexioned, sturdily built Balarama was serious and quick-tempered, while Krishna was cheerful and naughty. With time, he was also growing into a dark and slim youth.

Other than cowherds, all the gopis were also fond of him and could not resist it when he called out to them by playing on his flute.

Sometimes the gopis complained to Yashoda about his breaking their pots or eating up their butter. But they enjoyed that as well and felt bad if Krishna did not play pranks with them for long. They would miss his teasing and complain to Yashoda about that as well!

Radha especially adored him. Even on dark nights with rain pouring down, she would answer the call of Krishna's flute and go to meet him secretly. Radha-Krishna became a well-recognized pair.

Krishna and Narakasura

Bhoomi Devi or Mother Earth had a son named Naraka. Even though Naraka was the son of a goddess, he had the nature of a demon. Naraka was powerful and took pleasure in terrorizing the inhabitants of the three worlds.

One day, Narakasura heard that Lord Indra, the King of Devas, had thousands of divine elephants in his army.

'Devraj Indra has thousands of elephants! I must do something to acquire them!' thought the demon greedily. So he attacked the heavens!

Indra was helpless as he watched Naraka's demons plunder the heavens. Naraka himself began chasing the devas. While pursuing the devas, a glimmering object caught his eye. When he went closer, he realized that the glimmer came from Mother Aditi's (the mother of the devas) earrings! He attacked Mother Aditi and snatched away her earrings.

Now Indra, feeling humiliated at his loss and even worse that his mother was assaulted, wanted revenge. He knew that there was only one person who could teach Naraka a lesson. It was Krishna!

Indra told Krishna about the happenings and begged him for his help. 'O Lord, please help us as Narakasura has made our life hell! He has plundered heaven and also insulted Mother Aditi!' said Indra, helplessly.

Krishna was enraged that Naraka had laid his hands on Mother Aditi and declared that Naraka should be punished for his insolence. He then summoned Garuda (a giant eagle) and made way towards Naraka's fortress.

An impenetrable barrier of magical mountains surrounded Naraka's fortress. The mountains were such that a barrier would come up from any side that Krishna tried to enter the fortress. Krishna, unperturbed, hurled his mace at the barrier and shattered the entire mountain range in one blow. A downpour of magical weapons rained down on him. Krishna fired multiple arrows and destroyed all the weapons. In this manner, Krishna destroyed countless other magical barriers and finally reached Naraka's fortress.

Naraka's palace was guarded by the five-headed demon Mura. Mura hurled countless weapons at Krishna, but Krishna shot each one down with his bow and arrow. Then Krishna picked up his flying discus and hurled it towards Mura, slicing off his five heads. Mura fell to the ground dead.

Krishna challenged Naraka to battle and killed him easily. Bhoomi Devi then sang hymns in praise of Krishna and begged him to take Naraka's son Bhagdatta under his protection. Krishna placed Bhagdatta on the throne and then freed all of Naraka's prisoners. The gods showered Krishna with flowers from the heavens.

Krishna Goes to Mathura

Krishna performed many miracles. The stories of his miracles spread far and wide. Kamsa, Krishna's cruel maternal uncle heard all of this. He was worried. Then an idea struck him.

'If I can somehow bring Krishna to Mathura, my own land, he could be overpowered,' thinking so, Kamsa arranged for a wrestling match and invited Krishna and Balarama, Krishna's elder brother to participate.

Krishna knew that the time had come to put an end to Kamsa's treachery and accepted the invitation. And so, Krishna and Balarama went to Mathura.

While walking through the city of Mathura, they were met by a poor garland maker. He had heard of Krishna before. He was convinced that Krishna was the Lord himself incarnated. So he immediately ran towards Krishna and decorated him with flowers and fell at his feet. Krishna was greatly pleased and told him to ask for any boon.

'I am greatly pleased with you, my dear. Please make a wish which I can fulfil,' said Krishna smiling.

'Bless me so that I am kind to all living beings on this earth. Bless me so that I remain your devotee forever!' the garland maker said. Krishna granted the boon.

Krishna and Balarama finally reached the palace where the wrestling match was to take place. At the gate was a giant elephant called Kuvalayapida. This elephant was trained to trample and kill Krishna the moment it saw him.

When Krishna reached the palace gates, the elephant attacked him, but Krishna caught hold of the elephant's trunk, swirled it a hundred times and dashed it to the ground! Then, pulling out its tusks, Krishna and Balarama entered the wrestling arena with pride and enthusiasm. Seeing the two mighty boys, the crowd and other wrestlers trembled in fear.

The wrestlers Chanura and Mushtika challenged Krishna and Balarama respectively. Krishna and Chanura fought with each other, eager for victory. Fist against fist, elbow against elbow, head against head and chest against chest, they clashed. Whirling around, arm in arm, pushing away with a stroke of the hand, trying to strangle by embracing, throwing down on the ground, pushing forward and backward by all such means each tried to overpower the other. They

tried to hurt each other and win by throwing up, by lifting, by whirling, by pressing down and many such other tactics. Balarama fought with Mushtika in the same way.

The wrestlers fought valiantly but were defeated in the end by the two boys. Many other wrestlers challenged the two young boys but every single one of them was defeated in the end.

Finally, Krishna rushed at Kamsa. Kamsa drew out his sword and a great battle followed between the two. Eventually, Krishna dragged Kamsa throughout the arena and killed him.

Kamsa's eight brothers, furious on hearing about Kamsa's death came to fight Krishna, but Balarama killed them all.

At last, the kingdom of Mathura was free of the treacherous Kamsa. Krishna freed his mother and father Devaki and Vasudeva from the prison and crowned Ugrasena, Kamsa's father as the king of Mathura.

Krishna and Balarama continued to live in Mathura for a while, but eventually returned to Dwaraka where Krishna set up his kingdom.

The Panchajanya Conch

Once Krishna went to Sage Sandipani to study the scriptures. In three months, he had become well versed in them.

As he took his leave, Krishna asked the sage about his gurudakshina or fees.

'Free my son from the demon Panchajan. That would be my gurudakshina,' said the sage.

Panchajan was a shankhasur, a sea-creature in a giant conch-shell called the Panchajanya.

Once when sage Sandipani had gone to bathe in the pilgrimage spot of Prabhasa, Panchajan had grabbed hold of his young son, and taken him down with him.

Krishna went immediately to Prabhasa. He dived down to the depths of the sea, fought Panchajan and killed him. But unfortunately, Panchajanya had already killed Sandipani's son. Krishna went to the abode of Yam, the god of Death, and brought him back, alive.

'My fees are amply paid,' said Sage Sandipani, happily.

The conch-shell that the demon used to live in became Krishna's Panchajanya shankha. Every time he declared war on evil, he blew on it.

In Gokul, Krishna had played the flute. Now the conch-shell replaced it.

Krishna and Sudama

Sudama and Krishna were childhood friends. They first met at the ashram of Guru Sandipani. After few years, the boys completed their studies and went their separate ways.

When they grew up, Krishna married Rukmini and ruled Dwaraka. And Sudama married a poor brahmin girl and led a simple life.

Soon, children were born to Sudama and his wife. As the children grew older, the family's needs also grew, but the means didn't. Often, the family would sleep without food. Days passed like this. Sudama's wife could not bear to see their children hungry.

One day, she suggested to Sudama hesitantly, 'My Lord, you could ask your friend Krishna for help because he is very rich and powerful.' Sudama was not comfortable in seeking help from his friend. But his wife insisted for the sake of their children. 'I know that it hurts your self-respect to ask for help from your friend. But think about these little lives!'

Hearing this, Sudama agreed to go and see his friend but said that he would not ask him for anything.

Sudama's wife borrowed some roasted rice from a neighbour and wrapped it in a clean cloth and gave it to Sudama. Taking it, he left for Dwaraka.

Krishna was overjoyed on seeing Sudama. 'My friend, what kept you away from me for so long? Why didn't you meet me earlier?'asked Krishna, welcoming his old friend happily.

And then, he made Sudama sit down and washed his feet. Rukmini fanned him gently. Sudama was overwhelmed by the love that Krishna showered on him. He hesitated to give

Krishna the rice, thinking it to be a very small gift for someone like him. But Krishna read his mind and snatched it from his hand.

'Oh, roasted rice! My favourite!'exclaimed Krishna and ate a handful greedily.

Before he could take the second handful, Rukmini stopped him saying, 'One mouthful will give him all that he needs, My Lord.'

Next morning, Sudama left Dwaraka. His heart was full, though he did not ask for anything from Krishna.

'I know my wife will be upset for not asking Krishna for help. But I just couldn't do so after seeing his love,' thought Sudama.

As he approached his house, he saw a grand mansion. His wife and children came out of it wearing fine clothes and jewels. 'My Lord, look what your friend has done for us! He is so generous and he loves you so much!'

Sudama realized that Krishna had read his mind and knew about his condition. His devotion to Krishna increased even more.

Satyabhama

Satrajit, a chief of the Yadava clan, was a devoted friend of Surya, the Sun-god. As a mark of his devotion, Surya had given Satrajit a brilliant Syamantak mani or gem with special powers. It protected the country from droughts, diseases, fires, robberies and other disasters. It could also help to produce gold. But the condition was that only a noble and honest person could wear it on his body.

Satrajit once came to visit Krishna in Dwaraka. Everyone at Dwaraka was impressed by the glow of the gem he had adorned himself with. Even Krishna wanted Satrajit to gift it to him. Scared that Krishna would rob him off his gem, Satrajit passed it on to his brother Prasenjit.

Now Prasenjit was not a noble person at all. He could not carry the powerful jewel for long. One day, while out hunting, a lion pounced upon him and killed him. A huge bear then came upon the scene. It killed the lion and made off with the gem.

When Satrajit heard the report, he took the whole thing to be a plot of Krishna to get hold of the gem for himself.

To disprove this, Krishna went into the forest. Reaching the spot where Prasenjit and the lion lay dead, he saw the paw marks of a bear leading away from the scene.

Following them, he reached the bear's cave. After a long fight, Krishna killed the bear. The bear's daughter handed over the gem to Krishna, who handed it over to Satrajit himself.

On getting the Syamantak mani back, Satrajit was so pleased with Krishna that he gave his daughter Satyabhama's hand in marriage to him.

Rukmini

Bhishmak, the king of Vidarbha, had a son named Rukmi and a daughter named Rukmini. Princess Rukmini had heard of Krishna's killing the evil king Kamsa, and fell in love with him. Prince Rukmi for the same reason hated Krishna.

Jarasandha, the king of Magadha, and father-in-law of Kamsa, was an ally of Damghosh, the king of Chedi. Damghosh's son Shishupal had been brought up in Magadha like Jarasandha's own son.

Jarasandha suggested Shishupal to be the bridegroom for Princess Rukmini. Bhishmak agreed to the proposal, though Prince Rukmi opposed it.

The wedding arrangements were on. Suddenly Krishna arrived there with his elder brother Balarama, and carried Rukmini off! Prince Rukmi and Shishupal tried to get her back, but failed.

Krishna went on to have many wives, including Satyabhama, but Rukmini was the chief among them. She had ten sons and one daughter. The eldest son named Pradyumna grew up to be a prominent Yadava warrior.

Getting the Kalpavriksha

One day, Satyabhama was sulking to see all the other wives of Krishna go about with fragrant flowers from the Kalpavriksha (Tree of Desire) in Indra's own garden. Narada, the sage who was devoted to Vishnu, and had the power to fly between heaven and earth, had been visiting them. It was he who had brought the flowers for Krishna.

Krishna had given away the flowers to his wives. But somehow he had missed out Satyabhama!

'Why do you mind, dear Satyabhama?' asked Krishna when he found her sulking. 'I'll get you, not just a flower from the Kalpavriksha in Indra's garden, but the tree itself !'

Off he went to Indralok. Indra, the king of gods, did not want to part with his dear Kalpavriksha. It was a very special tree with the magical power of giving all the fruits that one could desire. It had been churned out of the Sea of Milk by gods and demons and Indra had taken it away for himself.He had planted it in Nandan-kanan, the garden of heaven, where it now blossomed.

There was a fight between Indra and Krishna. Indra was defeated. Krishna uprooted the Kalpavriksha from Indra's garden and brought it down for Satyabhama to plant in her own garden at Dwaraka.

Next to Rukmini, Satyabhama was the most important among Krishna's wives. She had seven sons, the eldest being named Bhanu.

The Battle of Kurukshetra

Hastinapur was a prosperous kingdom in the north of India, ruled by the renowned Kuru dynasty. But later this dynasty was ripped apart by conflict that led to a big battle on the plains of Kurukshetra.

King Shantanu of Hastinapur had a son named Devavrata, also known as Bhishma, who had taken a vow to never marry. Shantanu's two other sons had died early. Sage Vyasa had then blessed the Kuru family with three sons, Dhritarashtra, Vidura and Pandu. Dhritarashtra was born blind and Vidura was born to a maid of the palace.

So it was Pandu who became the king. However, due to a twist of fate, Pandu had to go away to the Himalayan forests with his wives Kunti and Madri. There, five sons were born to him through the blessings of gods Dharma, Pavana, Indra and the Ashwini kumaras. Three of them, Yudhisthira, Bheema and Arjuna were born to Kunti. Nakula and Sahadeva were born to Madri. These five sons were called Pandavas.

Back in the palace, Dhritarashtra became the king. He and his wife Gandhari had one hundred sons, called Kauravas, and one daughter. The eldest two sons were Duryodhana and Dushasana.

Pandu and Madri died in the forest. Kunti returned to the palace with the Pandavas. All the princes the hundred Kauravas and the five Pandavas were given rigorous training in archery, wrestling, mace-fight and other arts of warfare.

Everyone considered Yudhisthira to be the natural heir to the throne of Hastinapur, but Duryodhana hated his cousins, the Pandavas. He felt, that being the reigning king's son, he was the rightful heir.

Shakuni, Duryodhana's maternal uncle, fanned his hatred of the Pandavas. And blind Dhritarashtra was so fond of his son that he never corrected him.

Once Duryodhana had tried to poison and drown Bheema. Now, with Shakuni's help, he plotted to burn all five brothers alive in a house made of lac. The resourceful Pandavas were able to save themselves, but let the world believe that they were dead. Disguised as Brahmins, depending on charity, they moved from place to place.

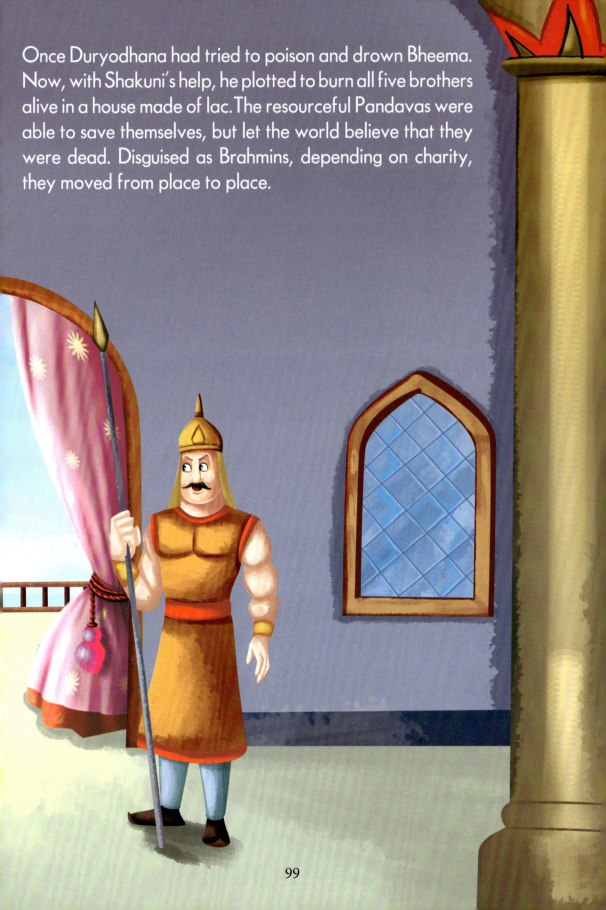

In the kingdom of Panchala, at an archery competition arranged by King Drupada, Arjuna won the hand of his daughter Draupadi, also called Panchali. As per Kunti's advice, Draupadi became wife to all five Pandavas.

Krishna, who was related to Kunti, was also there at the archery competition. He recognized the Pandavas in spite of their disguise.

Realizing that the Pandavas were not dead, Dhritarashtra called them back and gave them some forest area, called Khandavaprastha, as their share of the family property.

The Pandavas settled down there with their new bride Draupadi and began to develop the place. Arjuna, with his cousin Krishna, burnt down the Khandava forest. The Pandavas built an exquisite hall at Khandavaprastha, now called Indraprastha.

Duryodhana grew envious of Yudhisthira's increasing power and fame. His uncle Shakuni came out with another of his evil plans. Yudhisthira was challenged to a game of dice at Hastinapur, and was tricked

out of all his possessions his kingdom, wealth, brothers and even his wife. Eventually, Dhritarashtra set the Pandavas free to go back to Indraprastha.

But on Shakuni's advice, Duryodhana again invited Yudhisthira to a game of dice. This time the condition was that if Yudhisthira lost, he would hand over his kingdom to Duryodhana for twelve years and retire to the forest with his brothers and Draupadi. At the end of those twelve years, all of them would have to live somewhere in disguise for one year. If they were caught before the year was out, they would have to serve the term all over again.

This time too, Yudhisthira lost to Shakuni's trickery. With Draupadi and his brothers, he had to leave for the forests. Arjuna went to the

Himalayas and got the gods to give him some divine weapons that could be used against the Kauravas if there ever was a war against them.

At the end of twelve years, the Pandavas hid themselves in Viratanagara, the capital of the kingdom of Matsya, as employees of King Virata.

It so happened that a neighbouring king attacked the kingdom of Virata. King Virata set out with his soldiers, accompanied by his new

employees Yudhisthira, Bheema, Nakula and Sahadeva. Just then Kauravas came to Viratanagara and began to take away all the cattle that King Virata had. It was Arjuna, in his disguise as dance-master, who had to save the cattle.

By now one year of living in hiding was over. The Pandavas revealed their identity to King Virata. But Duryodhana said that by fighting in a way only Arjuna could have, he had given himself away before the year of hiding was fully over. By the terms and conditions of the second game of dice, the Pandavas were now due for another round of exile and hiding.

There were negotiations for peace, led by Krishna himself. But Duryodhana refused to yield. Finally Kauravas and Pandavas came to battle on the plains of Kurukshetra.

Arjuna's Dilemma

A mighty war began at the battlefield of Kurukshetra. The armies of Pandavas and Kauravas had assembled. All around there was uproar of soldiers shouting, conch shells blowing, horses neighing and elephants trumpeting.

Duryodhana was apprehensive due to the prowess of the Pandava army and Lord Krishna being on their side. However, he pacified himself by expressing the glories of his own army to his martial Guru Dronacharya.

Thus, starting with Bhishma, all warriors blew their conch shells to herald the beginning of the war. Krishna became Arjuna's charioteer and counsellor. He brought Arjuna's chariot to the front line for an overview. Seeing all his beloved relatives, like Guru Dronacharya, Guru Kripacharya, his uncles and cousins, including his grandfather, on the other side, Arjuna was overwhelmed with grief.

'How, can I fight my near and dear ones O Krishna! I cannot fight this battle. I do not wish any riches or kingdom. What use is victory if my loved ones are not there for me?'

Overcome with grief, Arjuna refused to fight even though he knew that Kauravas had wronged his family.

'O Krishna, war brings only misery and disaster. I cannot kill my kith and kin. Let them kill me instead!' Saying so, he dropped his bow and sank down in despair.

It was then that Krishna came forward and taught Arjuna how the righteous path was not always an easy one. One had to be willing to fight for what one believed to be right even if it meant sacrificing one's own life. This sermon came to be known as the Bhagavad Gita.

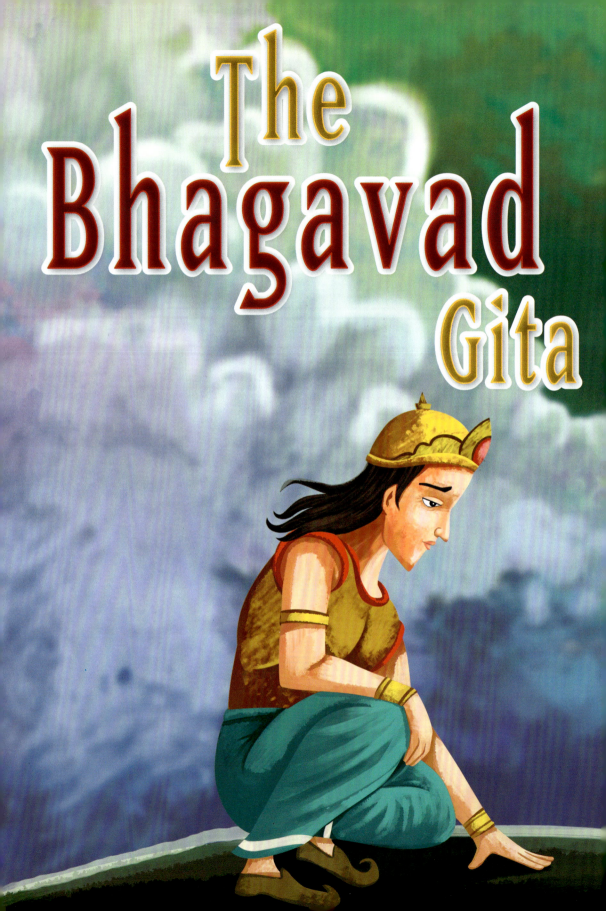

Krishna said, 'O Arjuna, let not this dilemma reign over your mind. Don't behave like a coward as your enemies are not thinking about your well-being. This war is no ordinary war. It is a Dharmayuddha, the battle of righteousness! It is a battle between good and evil!'

'May it be known to you that a person's dharma lies in performing their duty while the results should be left to God. To oppress others is a sin but to tolerate oppression is a far greater sin.

All those, whom you claim to be your relatives, are none but individual souls, unrelated to you! They are on their way to the ultimate destination

of uniting with the supreme Lord, the Brahma. So do not worry, and pick up your weapon and fight! That is what is ordained for you. Do not think of the consequences.'

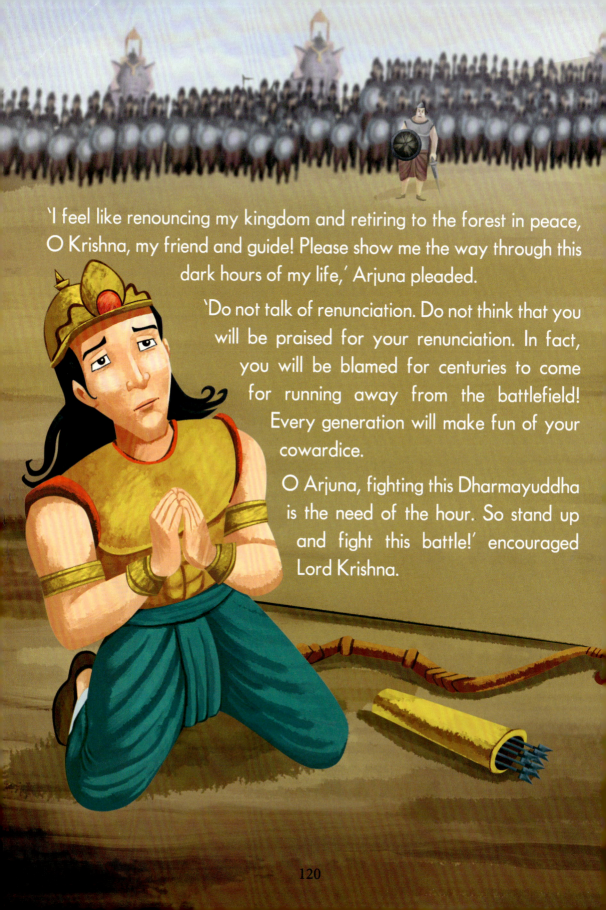

'I feel like renouncing my kingdom and retiring to the forest in peace, O Krishna, my friend and guide! Please show me the way through this dark hours of my life,' Arjuna pleaded.

'Do not talk of renunciation. Do not think that you will be praised for your renunciation. In fact, you will be blamed for centuries to come for running away from the battlefield! Every generation will make fun of your cowardice.

O Arjuna, fighting this Dharmayuddha is the need of the hour. So stand up and fight this battle!' encouraged Lord Krishna.

121

The Eternal Soul

Krishna further said, 'Those who are wise, lament neither for living nor for dead. Everything exists eternally. Although there is always some pain in losing our loved ones the wise undergo that pain with patience and tolerance. They carry on without letting grief overwhelm their lives and ruin their responsibilities.'

Krishna then explained the fundamental distinction between temporary material body and eternal spiritual soul.

'Soul is indestructible, immeasurable, unborn and eternal. Childhood, youth, old age and death are attributed to the body and not to the soul. The feelings of heat and cold are transitory. One should ignore them. The people about whom you are worried are mortal, perishable! So why lament?'

'Fight, O Kunti-putra, fight! Don't worry about their bodies, as they are already lifeless. What is real is the soul, and that is indestructible. The soul is never born and it never dies. Even if you kill them, their souls will be alive.'

'No weapon can cut a soul, no fire can burn it. Water cannot drench it, nor the wind can dry it. Death is simply a change of body for the soul, like a change of clothes. We, the eternal spiritual soul, have no reason for having grief over death of the temporary body. The elements that form the body and life return to nature after death and again form another body, another life. As such, there is no cause for grief.'

The Lord said, 'Know the truth, O Arjuna. Whoever is born has to die and whoever is dead has to be reborn. A man who has no knowledge, thinks that he is a body with a soul, but in reality it is a soul with a body! Lack of this knowledge is the cause of grief.'

'This knowledge about the souls is known as Brahmavidya. So my dear Arjuna, know yourself and be free forever.'

The Path of Karma

Krishna further reminded Arjuna that happiness comes only from right action, that is, duty. Arjuna's duty as a warrior was to protect the virtuous. Even if Arjuna were to die in the war, he would attain heaven as the reward of dutiful action.

The results of wise action are imperishable. The wise, therefore, strive for wise action with steady determination. This ultimate goal or enlightenment is best achieved by wise action or karmayoga in which one acts out of duty only, without personal attachment or expectation.'

Krishna also explained the reason for the need of devotional activities. If one does not fix his mind upon God, it will attach itself to sensory objects, leading to illusion. Engaging in devotional activities helps to

control one's senses. A true devotee has a steady mind and is indifferent towards good or evil.

Arjuna listened to Krishna patiently. At times he understood what the Lord said, and at times he didn't. He was a little puzzled.

'O Lord, I fail to understand your words. On one hand you say that all emotions and attachments should be abandoned and on the other you are urging me to fight a battle that involves a lot of passion and anger! You tell me to do my duty, but how can fighting my own relatives be my duty?'

Krishna explained, 'O Arjuna, do not confuse the path of knowledge with the path of karma or action. Everyone has to engage himself in some sort of work according to his qualities or nature. As a warrior, your duty is to fight the evil.'

'One must do one's duty without attachment, that is the key,' saying so Krishna smiled.

'Tell me, O Lord, what forces a man to commit sin?' asked Arjuna.

'Desire, dear Arjuna brings our downfall. It invites worries, sadness and sufferings along with it. It is desire that prevents us from seeing the soul or God within us or around us. O Arjuna, kill this enemy and be free!' Krishna answered.

Knowledge of God

Lord Krishna then mentioned two major paths to peace and happiness in life, 'One is that of sacrifice of one's material possessions, and the other is knowledge of self. Knowledge of self is purely a spiritual activity.

If someone's material sacrifice is not connected to any spiritual cause, then such sacrifice becomes simply materialistic. But if one performs sacrifice with a spiritual objective, then he makes a perfect sacrifice.

When we perform spiritual activities, we find that these are also divided into two namely, understanding of one's own self, and understanding the truth or the real nature of the Lord, which is eternal, all-knowing and blissful.'

Arjuna seemed puzzled. 'You and I are almost of the same age, O Lord. Then how is it that you know everything that has happened from the beginning of the creation?' he asked.

At this Krishna smiled and said, 'You and I have passed through many births. I know them all, while you do not. Whenever there is a decline in the righteousness in the world, I manifest myself for the protection of the virtuous and destruction of the evil doers. I am reborn throughout the ages. One who has the knowledge and understanding of this reality is liberated. After leaving this mortal body, such souls never come back to this temporary world of miseries.'

'Tell me more about knowledge, O Lord,' asked Arjuna, now more curious.

'Even if you are the most sinful person, you can burn all the sins with knowledge! Knowledge is like a purifier.'

'And how can one attain knowledge?' asked Arjuna.

'A man who has full control of his senses, who is truly devoted to spiritual practice and is full of faith, attains knowledge. So Arjuna, shed all your doubts! Doubts come from ignorance.'

Conscious Action

Krishna continued, 'One who neither hates nor desires the fruits of his actions is known to be always renounced. One who works in devotion, though he is always working, is a man who is never entangled. While the one who is greedy for fruits, become entangled. One who acts with knowledge but inwardly renounces the fruits, attains peace, detachment and bliss.'

The Lord explained that it is important to think about the result of any action before taking it up. When we choose an action, we also choose its result. That's why work or any action has to be done for the welfare of all and not just to satisfy a desire or personal gain.

Conquering the Mind

Arjuna was listening patiently till now. But he still looked perplexed, 'O Lord, you have explained to me about the path of spiritual knowledge and the path of selfless action. Which is better?'

Both the paths lead to supreme bliss. But Lord Krishna considered the path of selfless action, or service to humanity without attachment to its results, as the best path for most people.

Then he explained how it was important to engage one's body, mind and soul in the service of Lord. The mind is the most difficult to control and one has to conquer it, otherwise, lust, anger, greed, hatred, etc would always distract and deviate the person. The conqueror of mind automatically follows the direction of the Supreme Lord.

'How should man control his mind, O Krishna?' was the expected question from Arjuna.

'Man can control himself through meditation. The third path to God is the yoga of meditation,' was Krishna's response.

One who is united with God is called a yogi. A yogi has control over his mind, senses and desires. He is free from anger and greed. He sees God in everything and everything in God.

In order to meditate, sitting in a quiet place, one should hold one's body, neck and head erect and stare steadily at the tip of one's nose with a calm mind.

Regulation of the habits of eating, sleeping, recreation and work, also helps to de-stress and relax. Continuous practice of this results in controlling our senses and desires better.

Attaining the Lord

Arjuna finally understood how to detach his mind from worldly pleasures through meditation.

'Now, I will tell you how to attach your mind to me. Meditate on me and you shall know me as the repository of all power and divinity the soul of all,' declared Krishna.

Arjuna listened carefully as Krishna carried on, 'Earth, water, air, fire, ether, mind, intelligence, constitute the material energy, and the living entity belongs to another superior energy. I am the source of all these energies.'

'The taste of water, light of the sun and the moon, the sound Om, the ability in man, the fragrance of the earth, the heat in fire, the strength of the strong, the intelligence of the intelligent all represent me! I am the eternal seed of all beings. All beings evolve from me and dissolve in me. I am the source of the entire creation. Only by surrendering to me, one can overcome all the hurdles in life.'

Lord Krishna further continued, 'The kind of thoughts one has during the course of his life accumulate to influence his thoughts at the time of his death. Whatever state of being one is at the time of death, he attains that without fail. The present life creates one's next life. So one should always contemplate on God.'

'How should a person contemplate on God?' asked Arjuna.

'It is very easy for my devotees to attain me at the time of their death. Simply by performing devotional service they reach my eternal abode!' Krishna replied.

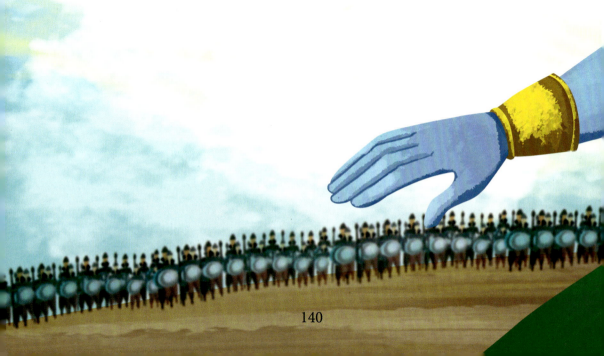

The Supreme Knowledge

Arjuna was listening intently all this while. Sometimes he understood what Krishna said and sometimes he questioned.

'My dear Arjuna, I shall impart to you the most confidential knowledge, knowing which, you shall be relieved of the miseries of existence,' said Lord Krishna.

142

'My unmanifested form pervades this entire universe. Although I am the maintainer of all living entities and although I am everywhere, I am not a part of this cosmic manifestation, for I am the very source of creation! The whole cosmic order is under me, yet, I am ever detached from all these material activities.

I am the ritual, the sacrifice the offering to the ancestors, the healing herb, the transcendental chant. I am the butter and the fire and the offering. I am the father of this universe, the mother, the support and the grandsire. I am the object of knowledge, the purifier and the syllable O. I am also the Rig, the Sama, the Atharva and the Yajur Vedas.

I am the goal, the sustainer, the master, the witness, the abode, the refuge and the dearest friend. I am the creation and the annihilation, the basis of everything.

143

Those who worship the demigods will take birth among the demigods; those who worship the ancestors will go to the ancestors; those who worship ghosts and spirits will take birth among such beings; and those who worship me, will live with me!'

Even if one commits the most abominable action, if he decides to engage in devotional service to me, he is to be considered saintly because he has made the right decision. He quickly becomes righteous and attains lasting peace. O son of Kunti, my devotee never perishes!'

The Omnipresent Krishna

Arjuna heard Krishna, mesmerized. He felt blessed to hear the glories of Krishna. He also felt very proud that he had such a magnificent friend and guide during his time of need to show him the way.

Krishna continued, 'I am present everywhere. Everything in this world moves and happens due to my will. All emotions like intellect, wisdom, forgiveness, truth, self-control, joy, sorrow, fear, self-control, charity and the like all these originate from me.

Anything extraordinarily beautiful and glorious should be considered as a fragmental manifestation of my splendour! All things exist due to my entering into them as Supersoul.' Saying this, Lord Krishna paused.

Arjuna, who was awestruck by his friend's revelations said, 'O Lord of the Lords, you are the prime deity, the unborn and all-pervading; I believe in you. It is true that neither the gods nor the demons can describe your divine glory. Only you can describe your divinity.

Forgive me as my mind still wanders through numerous confusions. Please do tell me in what particular forms should I perceive you? Please tell me once more in detail about your glory for my mind is yet not satisfied.'

Lord Krishna smiled at Arjuna's earnest pleadings.

'My friend, there is no limit to my magnitude. I reside in the hearts of all beings! I am the bright sun among all the celestial bodies; I am the Indra (king of gods) among the gods; I am the life-force in all beings; I am the Brihaspati among the priests; I am the ocean among the water bodies; I am Narada among the celestial sages; I am Varuna among the water gods; I am the wind in nature; I am Vasuki among all the serpents; I am the Ganges among the rivers; I am Rama!

Always know my dear Arjuna that I am the beginning, the middle and the end of all creations. I am the endless time; I am the wisdom in all beings; and I am in you among the Pandavas!

Always remember that every glorious creature whether living or non-living are parts of my existence. Know me to be all pervasive and omnipresent holding the universe in my divine power!'

The Cosmic Form of Krishna

The revelations of Krishna regarding his omnipresence had amazed Arjuna.

'O dear Lord of the universe, I want to thank you for your kindness and your sacred words. All my confusions are cleared now. But Lord, I wish to see your divine form. If you consider me suitable of beholding your eternal and imperishable form, please do reveal it to me.' Arjuna bowed his head and pleaded.

Hearing this, Krishna smiled and said, 'O brother Arjuna, I have innumerable divine forms of various colours. But how will you see them with your mortal eyes? For that, I will grant you divine vision.'

And so, Arjuna was bestowed divine vision. The next moment, Krishna came into his 'Vishwaroop' form, which was an unlimited, blazing, effulgent, universal form.

Arjuna, was stunned to see the cosmic form of Krishna. With folded hands, he offered prayers.

He saw the magnificent Lord Krishna having many faces on all sides, dressed in divine ornaments, emitting brilliant light and carrying celestial weapons. All around there was a strong, sweet fragrance of sandalwood.

The cosmic form of Krishna was so huge in size that he filled the space between the heaven and earth.

Arjuna also saw that the whole universe was part of his body! Lord Brahma was seated on the lotus flower and Lord Shiva with his serpents was also there. There were many other gods in Krishna's cosmic body.

Arjuna said, 'Lord, I have realized that you are the creator and the destroyer of all things! You possess eternal power.' As he was speaking, he saw all the gods and goddesses entering Krishna's divine body. He also saw Dhritarashtra's sons entering the Lord's mouth.

Seeing this, Arjuna asked nervously, 'Who are you and what is your mission, as all these people are entering your mouth to be destroyed!'

'Arjuna, understand that I am Kaal or Time, the destroyer of the world! I will destroy these people even without you. You feel that you will kill them but the reality is that I have already killed them,' Krishna responded.

At this, Arjuna begged for forgiveness. 'O merciful Lord, please forgive my mistakes as I did not know your real power. Please show me your original form O Lord, the form of Vishnu.' Arjuna wished to see the form that he had always worshipped.

Krishna manifested his four-armed form of Vishnu and then resumed his original two-armed form that was so very beautiful and dear to Arjuna.

Devotional Path

Arjuna was listening attentively to Krishna all this while. Seeing this, Krishna said, 'Till now I have explained about the path of knowledge and the path of action. There is yet another path through which one can attain me and that is the path of devotion.'

But after seeing the cosmic form of the Lord, Arjuna wanted to know which form should be worshipped - the formless, cosmic one, or the form of Krishna.

Krishna told Arjuna that worship of God with a form with faith was easier and better for most people. But a true devotee had faith in everything the formless God and God with a form such as Rama, Krishna, Hanuman, Shiva, Devi, etc.

A true devotee would be constantly engaged sometimes chanting, sometimes reading books about Krishna, or sometimes cooking prasadam or cleaning the temple or the dishes. Whatever he would do, he would not let a single moment pass without devoting his activities to Krishna. 'Tell me, O divine friend, what are the qualities of a true devotee?' asked Arjuna.

With a smile Krishna replied patiently, 'A true devotee is never disturbed in any circumstance, nor is he envious of anyone. He thinks that one is acting as his enemy due to his own past misdeeds, thus it is better to suffer than to protest. Whenever a devotee is in trouble, he thinks that it is the Lord's mercy upon him that he is not getting all the punishment he deserves. A devotee is also always kind to everyone, even to his enemy. He is tolerant, and he is satisfied with whatever comes by the grace of the Lord.'

A devotee for whom no one is put into difficulty and who is not disturbed by anxiety, who is steady in happiness and distress, is very dear to me. One who neither grasps pleasure or grief, who neither laments nor desires, is very dear to me. A pure devotee is neither happy nor distressed over material gain and loss. If he loses anything that is very dear to him, he does not lament. He is prepared to accept all kinds of risks for the satisfaction of the Lord. Such a devotee is very dear to me!'

Creation and Creator

Arjuna sat at the feet of Lord Krishna, absorbing his every word.

Krishna explained that the whole world, including our body, is made of five basic elements: earth, water, fire, air and ether. We have eleven senses: five sense organs (nose, tongue, eye, skin and ear); five organs of action (mouth, hand, leg, anus and urethra); and a mind.

158

We smell through our nose, taste through our tongue, see through the eyes, feel touch through skin, and hear through our ears. We also have a sense of feeling by which we feel pain and pleasure. All these give our body what it needs to work. The soul inside our body is also called Prana. It supplies power to the body to do all the work. When it leaves the body, we die.

There are six changes of the body, as the body is born, it grows, it stays, it produces by-products, then begins to decay, and at the last stage it vanishes. Therefore, the body is a non-permanent material object.

This body is made by material nature under the direction of God. Whatever one is supposed to do, either for happiness or for distress, one is forced to do because of the bodily constitution.

The Three Modes of Material Nature

Lord Krishna said again, 'Now I shall enlighten you about the supreme wisdom, the best of all knowledge.'

'The total material substance, called Brahma, is the source of birth, and it is that Brahma that I saturate making possible the births of all living beings, O son of Kunti. Everything that takes place in this world is due to the combination of the body and the soul.

Material nature consists of the three modes (gunas) goodness (sattva), passion (rajas) and ignorance (tamas). When the living entity comes in contact with nature, he or she becomes habituated by these modes and acts under the spell of the three modes of material nature.

Under the influence of the mode of goodness, one does good and right actions; under the influence of the mode of passion, one becomes selfish; and under the influence of the mode of ignorance, one does bad things or becomes lazy. Laziness destroys a person. Passion ties him to the world. Goodness frees him from the grasp of passion and laziness, but it cannot give him spiritual knowledge. When a person is able to transcend these three modes, he can become free from birth, death, old age and their distresses and can enjoy nectar even in this life.'

At this Arjuna asked thoughtfully, 'O my dear Lord, please tell me how does a man transcend these modes of nature?'

Krishna smiled and said, 'He who is unaffected by changes in material reactions, who regards pleasure and pain alike, who looks upon a stone and a piece of gold with an equal eye, who is unchanged in honour and dishonour, who treats friend and foe alike, such a person is said to have transcended the modes of nature.

Such people always engage in full devotional service, do not fall down in any circumstance and they at once transcend the modes of material nature. They actually come to the level of Brahma!'

The Eternal Tree of Creation

Lord Krishna said, 'The involvement of man with this material world is like a banyan tree. For one who is engaged in materialistic activities, there is no end to the banyan tree. He wanders from one branch to another. The tree of this material world has no end, and for one who is attached to this tree, there is no possibility of liberation from the chain of birth and death.

The problem lies in the fact that the real form of this tree cannot be perceived in this world. No one can understand where it ends, where it begins, or where its foundation is. But with determination one must cut down this tree with the weapon of detachment. After detaching one's own self, one must seek that eternal place from which no one ever returns and that place is me!'

'But Lord it is not easy to detach and surrender to you! Please explain this to me,' asked Arjuna thoughtfully.

At this, Krishna smiled. 'When one is free from illusion caused by pride, he can begin the process of surrender. Pride is due to illusion.

Although one is born in the world, lives for a brief time and then passes away, yet he has the foolish notion that he is the lord of the world. The whole world lives under this impression. People think that the land, this

earth, belongs to human society, and they have divided the land under the false impression that they are the owners! When one is freed from such a false notion, he becomes free!

One has to cultivate knowledge of what is actually his own and what is not. And, when one has an understanding of things as they are, he becomes free from happiness and distress, pleasure and pain. He becomes full in knowledge; then it is possible for him to surrender to me!'

Krishna continued, 'I am seated in everyone's heart, and from me come remembrance, knowledge and forgetfulness. I am situated as Paramatma in everyone's heart, and it is from me that all activities are initiated.'

Lord Krishna thus imparted the most secret knowledge to Arjuna and revealed the eternal truths one by one.

Arjuna like a true devotee kept absorbing Krishna's words of wisdom. He finally understood that the creation is changeable and does not last forever. It has a limited lifespan. The soul or Brahma does not change and is eternal. Krishna is the Para Brahma or the Supreme Being. He is the source of everything in the universe.

Nature of People

'Dear Arjuna, so far we have discussed about the soul, the body and the Supreme Power. Now I shall tell you about the people in this world. There are two types of people in this world good or divine and bad or demonic,' said Krishna.

He further said, 'The qualities of a good person are honesty, nonviolence, truthfulness, freedom from anger, kindness, gentleness, modesty, forgiveness and freedom from envy and greed.

And arrogance, pride, jealousy, selfishness, anger, greed, harshness, ungratefulness and violence are bad qualities that lead a person away from God, O son of Kunti!'

Then Krishna went on to say that most people have both good and bad qualities. Getting rid of bad habits and cultivating good ones is necessary for spiritual progress. And ended by saying, 'Do not worry, O son of Pandu, for you are born with the divine qualities!'

Arjuna asked, 'O mighty-armed one, I wish to understand the difference between renunciation or sannyas and selfless work or karma yoga.'

At this, the Supreme Lord replied, 'To walk away from family, home and possessions and living in a cave or forest is not renunciation.

A karma yogi gives up selfish attachment to the fruits of his work, while a sannyasi does not work for any personal gain.

One's prescribed duties must be performed with this thought. We all must perform our duties well for the benefit of the entire humanity. O brave warrior, realize your duty and act accordingly! You are a warrior and you should respond to the call of time.'

Division of Labour

Lord Krishna further explained that according to the Vedas, human beings were divided into four universal types of human labour. These four divisions — brahmin, kshatriya, vaishya and shudra — were based on the mental, intellectual and physical abilities of people.

Those who were interested in learning, teaching, preaching, and guiding people in spiritual matters were called brahmins or intellectuals.

Those who could defend the country, establish law and order, prevent crime, and administer justice were called kshatriyas, the warriors.

Those who were good in farming, cattle-raising, business, trade, finance, commerce and industry were known as vaishyas or businessmen.

Those who were very good in service and labour work were classed as shudras or workers.

Arjuna's next question was, 'How can anybody living and working in society attain liberation?'

Krishna responded thus, 'Work becomes worship when done as a service to the Lord and without selfish attachment to the results. If you work honestly for which you are suited you attain God.

Brahmins, kshatriyas, vaishyas and shudras work in accordance with their modes of nature.

174

The brahmins work through peacefulness, self-control, austerity, purity, tolerance, honesty, wisdom, knowledge, and religiousness.

Heroism power, determination, resourcefulness, courage in battle, generosity, and leadership are the qualities of the kshatriyas.

Farming cattle raising and business are the qualities of work for the vaishyas, and for the shudras.

By following the qualities of work, every man can become perfect. So my dear Arjuna, by your nature, you will have to be engaged in warfare.'

Then the Lord spoke again, 'O conqueror of wealth, Arjuna, have you heard this attentively with your mind? And are your illusions and ignorance now dispelled?'

Arjuna said, 'My dear Krishna, my illusion is gone and I stand firm and free from doubt. Now I am prepared to act according to your instructions.'

Krishna called out, 'AWAKE Arjuna! Get hold of your bow and fight for the noble cause. The battlefield beckons you!'

Hearing Krishna's mighty call, Arjuna felt new energy flowing into him. He picked up his weapons and got ready to fight. Amidst the sound of the conch, the neighing of war-horses, the trumpeting of war elephants, and the war cries raised by the soldiers, Arjuna stepped forward to fight in the name of justice.

'I will O Lord. My doubts have cleared and I have gained new knowledge.'

Saying this, Arjuna pulled the bowstring and the whole battlefield reverberated with its mighty TWANG! And so, began the mighty war of Kurukshetra, the war of good and evil!

Krishna in the Kurukshetra War

The Kurukshetra war began every day with Krishna blowing his Panchajanya conch.

Bhishma was the first army-chief of the vast Kaurava army, inflicting severe losses upon the Pandava side. Krishna had said that he would not take up arms in this battle. But Bhishma fought so ably that Krishna leapt down from the charioteer's seat and rushed at him with his Sudarshan chakra.

Bhishma put aside his bow and arrow and welcomed Krishna with folded palms. Arjuna jumped down from the chariot, and stopped Krishna.

Later Krishna kept telling Arjuna that he was not being tough enough with Bhishma. He reminded Arjuna that however terrible he may feel about it, but he had to keep his vow of killing Bhishma. Finally Arjuna used Shikhandi as a cover and shot Bhishma down to fall on a bed of arrows.

After Bhishma, it was Dronacharya who was the army-chief of the Kauravas. Now Krishna aided Arjuna in many ways, though he never exactly fought for the Pandavas. He drove the chariot so swiftly through such routes that Drona could never get too close to Arjuna. When the horses were tired, he let them have rest and a drink of water, and even massaged them. But sometimes, he came to Arjuna's rescue in more direct ways.

When King Bhagdatta shot the Vaishnavastra at Arjuna, Krishna came in front of Arjuna, and took it's blow upon himself.

When young Abhimanyu was killed unfairly by Jayadratha, it was Krishna who went to the camp to break the news to his mother Subhadra, and wife Uttara, who at that time was carrying Abhimanyu's baby. Krishna left them under Draupadi's care, and hurried back to the battlefield.

Arjuna had vowed to kill Jayadratha by sunset the next day. But Jayadratha had gone into hiding, so that Arjuna could not find him before the sun had set. This time, using his magical powers, Krishna created an illusion of darkness. Jayadratha thought that the sun had gone down, and came out from where he was hiding. Arjuna then shot out an arrow that cut off his head.

Karna, friend of Duryodhana and archrival of Arjuna, had a spear named Eka-purush-ghatini. It would kill, and never fail to do so, but only once. It could not be used again. Karna meant to use it on Arjuna and kept it with great care. Krishna pushed Ghatotkach, Bheema's son from demoness Hidimba, to come face-to-face with Karna. Ghatotkach fought so well that Karna had to use the Eka-purush-ghatini on him. Krishna was jubilant because now the weapon could no longer be used on Arjuna.

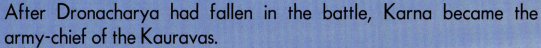

After Dronacharya had fallen in the battle, Karna became the army-chief of the Kauravas.

On the seventeenth day of the battle, Karna and Arjuna came face-to-face. Whenever Karna was at a disadvantage, Krishna advised Arjuna to seize the opportunity and kill Karna. Finally, the wheel of Karna's chariot got stuck in the slushy ground. In the name of the right conduct in war, Karna asked Arjuna for some time. But Krishna reminded him of the many times he had broken the code of conduct, and made Arjuna lose no time in killing Karna while he was still trying to lift up his chariot's wheel.

Shalya became the next army-chief of the Kauravas. 'Don't spare him because he is the maternal uncle of Nakula and Sahadeva,' Krishna advised the Pandavas on the eighteenth and last day of the battle.

After Shalya fell to Yudhisthira, a mace-fight took place between Duryodhana and Bheema. It was Krishna who suggested that Bheema should not stick to the code of right conduct, but fight to kill.Finally, Bheema hit Duryodhana below the waist and broke his knees.

Later at night Ashvatthama and a few others stealthily entered the Pandava camp and killed Draupadi's sons in their sleep. Draupadi sent Bheema out to take revenge on Ashvatthama who threw the Brahmashiras, a terrible weapon, at Bheema. Ultimately, it was the

baby within Abhimanyu's widow Uttara, who took the brunt of it. It was stillborn. But Krishna brought it back to life, and it was he who became the king of Hastinapur after Yudhisthira.

The Kaurava camp, in spite of having Krishna's Narayani Sena, was utterly defeated. Gandhari, the mother of the hundred Kaurava princes, cursed Krishna for this. 'You will die friendless and without help, in a manner petty and unworthy. Yadava men will kill one another and their widows will lament just as women are doing now at Kurukshetra,' she said.

End of Krishna's Leela

Years later, when King Yudhisthira and his brothers were all very old, the entire clan of Yadavas died of in-fighting, and their womenfolk were left lamenting. The city of Dwaraka, which had once been their refuge from attacks on Mathura, sank into the sea. The great serpent Sheshnag, who had been living within Balarama, came out of his mouth and left for the sea.

Krishna sat by himself at a deserted spot, and from a distance a hunter, named Jara could only see his pink foot. Taking it to be a deer, he shot at it, and hit Krishna instead.

Krishna bore no grudge against Jara. He felt that his task on earth had been completed, and happily ended his leela and returned to his abode, the Vishnulok.